Contents

LLANGOLLEN RAILWAY
NORTH WALES FOR SCENERY

Introduction

Title page: **LLANGOLLEN** Former Great Western '1400' Class 0-4-2 tank No 1450 stands ready to make a departure from Llangollen, resplendent in its unlined GWR livery. Locomotives of this class were first introduced by the GWR in 1932, and by 1936 a total of 75 had been built. The locomotives featured auto equipment for working with Great Western auto-coaches and were used widely on branch-line passenger services. *Peter Townsend*

Above: **RIVER SIDING** Running adjacent to the River Dee, Great Western 'Manor' Class 4-6-0 No 7822 *Foxcote Manor* climbs away from Llangollen at the head of a goods train. Although this section of the railway would appear to be double track, that is not actually the case; the track on the left is used for the storage of coaching stock and is often referred to locally as River Siding.

Front cover: **BERWYN** No 7822 *Foxcote Manor* prepares to make a departure from the distinctive Berwyn station, which stands high above the River Dee. A 'Cambrian Coast Express' headboard is carried by the locomotive; this named train could once be seen running from London and over the Cambrian line between Shrewsbury and Aberystwyth.

The Llangollen Railway, which today runs trains between Llangollen and Corwen, has almost completed its objectives of reinstating this part of the one-time Ruabon Junction to Barmouth route. The construction of a new terminus station in Corwen will complete the ambitions of the preservation society; access to the original station site was unrealistic due to the raising of the level of a road surface in the town since the closure of the line by British Railways in the 1960s, making it impractical to bridge it.

This preserved standard gauge North Wales route is popular with both railway enthusiasts and tourists visiting the Principality, and in recent times has been host to a wide range of guest steam locomotives, many of which feature in this publication.

The spirit of the line's former owner, the Great Western Railway, is still very much in evidence, with examples of former GWR locomotives and rolling stock contributing strongly to the formation of trains seen in action along the line today.

Although it would seem that further extension of the railway's running line in the future is not currently a valid prospect, the way ahead should see the Llangollen Railway go from strength to strength as it consolidates its position, operating heritage trains in this most scenic of Welsh locations.

Llangollen station

LLANGOLLEN station was once owned by the Great Western Railway and the presence of the station's former operator is clear to see here as '5600' Class 0-6-2 tank locomotive No 5643 takes on water at the water crane located on Platform 2. The sole surviving 'Dukedog' Class 4-4-0, No 9017, a visitor from the Bluebell Railway, prepares to depart from Platform 1 with a passenger service.

LLANGOLLEN Another sole surviving example of a GWR locomotive from the steam era is this railmotor; originally built in 1908, it was converted to an auto-trailer in 1935. It was fully restored to its original form at the Great Western Society's Didcot Railway Centre base and, following completion of the work in 2011, ran for the very first time in 75 years.

Above: **LLANGOLLEN** A mixed train comprising a British Railways Mark 1 suburban coach and goods vehicles makes a Platform 2 departure, with 1937-built '6400' Class 0-6-0 pannier tank No 6430 leading the way.

Left: **LLANGOLLEN** station occupies a restricted area adjacent to the River Dee. The first station in the town was located to the east of what we see today, with the current site eventually evolving due to the extension of the line to Corwen. Having just a single platform when it opened in 1865, a second was added to allow for the doubling of the line from Ruabon in 1898.

Above: **LLANGOLLEN** The bridge joining the two platforms was built following the addition of the second platform, and due to the restricted area occupied by the station it is unusual in overhanging the river.

Above: **LLANGOLLEN** Signal Box is the original one and is located at the eastern end of Platform 1, controlling train movements in and around the station.

Left: **LLANGOLLEN** The road bridge to the east of the station once crossed the tracks to and from Ruabon, but today it is blocked off, with buffer stops marking the termination of Llangollen Railway operations. It is currently unlikely that services will ever be reinstated to the east of Llangollen.

Left: **LLANGOLLEN** A 'Cambrian Coast Express' headboard is carried by No 4566, a '4500' Class 'Small Prairie' tank locomotive built at Swindon by the Great Western Railway in 1924. The 2-6-2T and 'Manor' Class 4-6-0 No 7822 *Foxcote Manor* are moving to join the train standing at Platform 1.

Below left: **LLANGOLLEN** The 'Small Prairie' and 'Manor' combination make a Llangollen departure.

Below: **LLANGOLLEN** On departing from the station, trains encounter a cutting as they pass the locomotive department, which is located above the running line on the site of the former Llangollen goods depot. Visiting 'Manor' Class 4-6-0 No 7820 *Dinmore Manor* is seen shortly after making a Platform 1 departure.

Left: **LLANGOLLEN** A former LMS locomotive, Class 5 2-6-0 No 42968, visiting from the Severn Valley Railway, makes a Platform 1 departure.

Below left: **LLANGOLLEN** These LMS 2-6-0s were introduced in 1933 during William Stanier's tenure as Chief Mechanical Engineer. No 42968 emerged new from Crewe Works in 1934, and is today the sole survivor of this once 40-strong class of locomotives.

Below: **LLANGOLLEN** Following its departure from Platform 2, Llangollen Railway-based '5101' Class 'Large Prairie' tank locomotive No 5199 makes progress as it climbs away from the station with a train of British Railways Mark.1 suburban coaching stock.

Leaving Llangollen

Right: **LLANGOLLEN** Former Stanier LMS Class 5 4-6-0 No 45337 climbs away from Llangollen towards Llangollen Goods Junction as it runs adjacent to River Siding. The latter is used for stabling coaching stock, but because these shots were taken during a major gala event the siding is empty, giving the impression of a double-track formation.

Below: **LLANGOLLEN** Taken from a higher vantage point, this shot clearly shows the River Dee as the backdrop to '5101' Class 'Large Prairie' No 5199.

Below right: **LLANGOLLEN** No 5526 is also captured adjacent to River Siding as it climbs away from Llangollen. This is an example of the Great Western '4575' Class, a development of the '4500' Class 'Small Prairie' 2-6-2Ts. No 5526 is normally based at the South Devon Railway and is seen during a visit to the Llangollen Railway.

In April 2009 the Betton Grange Society organised and staged 'Steel, Steam & Stars II', a nine-day gala event. It included in its list of guest locomotives the only two surviving former Great Western Railway outside-framed 4-4-0s, Nos 9017 and 3440 *City of Truro*.

The Betton Grange Society is based at the Llangollen Railway and is actively pursuing its aim of building a Great Western 'Grange' Class 4-6-0, there being no surviving members of the class in existence.

Right: **LLANGOLLEN** No 9017 climbs away from Llangollen. A visitor from the Bluebell Railway, this 4-4-0 normally carries *Earl of Berkeley* nameplates. The '3200' 'Earl' Class locomotives were built at Swindon between 1936 and 1939, and were Collett rebuilds consisting of former 'Duke' Class boilers mounted on former 'Bulldog' Class frames. As a result the class became nicknamed 'Dukedogs'. Thirty examples emerged from Swindon Works, with No 9017 entering traffic as No 3217 in 1938.

The 'Earl' names were eventually reallocated to 'Castle' Class locomotives, leaving the 4-4-0s unnamed. They eventually became the '9000' Class and were renumbered; this engine, the only surviving 'Dukedog', was withdrawn from service in 1960 as No 9017.

Left: **LLANGOLLEN** Today *City of Truro* is part of the National Collection, housed at the National Railway Museum in York. Although the locomotive is no longer operational, back in 2009 it was full of life and still in full steam as it is seen climbing away from Llangollen.

Left: **LLANGOLLEN** Carrying unlined LMS black livery and the LMS number 12322, this 0-6-0 visitor to the railway dates from the 19th century. Built at Horwich Works, it entered traffic with the Lancashire & Yorkshire Railway in 1896. Referred to as Class '27' and designed by John Aspinall, a total of 484 class members were built between 1889 and 1918, with this example being the sole survivor. It is seen here lifting coaching stock from River Siding at the beginning of the day's operations during a gala event.

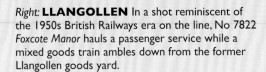

Right: **LLANGOLLEN** In a shot reminiscent of the 1950s British Railways era on the line, No 7822 *Foxcote Manor* hauls a passenger service while a mixed goods train ambles down from the former Llangollen goods yard.

Opposite page: **LLANGOLLEN LOCO SHED** occupies what was once Llangollen goods yard, and provides a base for the Locomotive Department, with everything from major overhaul to running repairs and the stabling of the running fleet being carried out here. The Betton Grange Society can also be found here as it carries out its aim of building a 'Grange' Class 4-6-0, thus filling a gap in the range of preserved former GWR 4-6-0 locomotives. No 7822 *Foxcote Manor* is seen here being prepared for its day's duties.

This page: **LLANGOLLEN LOCO SHED** This sequence of three shots shows No 5199, the resident '5101' Class 'Large Prairie' 2-6-2 tank locomotive, being prepared for its day's work (*top left*) before moving off shed (*below left*). Finally we see it proceeding down the incline towards Llangollen Goods Junction prior to reversing into River Siding, where it will be coupled to the coaching stock visible there. The completed train will then proceed to Llangollen station where it will eventually become a timetabled departure along the line to Corwen.

Llangollen goods junction

Above: **LLANGOLLEN GOODS JUNCTION** *Foxcote Manor* occupies the 'centre road' at Goods Junction prior to reversing down to Llangollen station with its mixed goods train. The middle track of the three at this location is used as a loop to allow incoming trains from the west to cross those leaving Llangollen on the track closest to the signal box.

Above: **LLANGOLLEN GOODS JUNCTION** Ex-LMS Stanier Class 5 (more commonly referred to as a 'Black Five') No 44806 approaches Goods Junction's home signal with its train from Llangollen. The line to the left gives access to the Llangollen Railway's Locomotive Department.

Right: **LLANGOLLEN GOODS JUNCTION** A train departs from Goods Junction bound for Carrog in 2009. Note the position of the starter signal here, located adjacent to the eastern end of the signal box.

Left: **LLANGOLLEN GOODS JUNCTION** The signalman looks out of the signal box as GWR '4500' Class 'Small Prairie' tank locomotive No 5526 passes with its westbound train from Llangollen. The section starter signal is out of sight in this shot, being located on the other side of the box.

Below left: **LLANGOLLEN GOODS JUNCTION** The 'Dukedog' 4-4-0, visiting from the Bluebell Railway, passes the signal box with a mixed goods train during an intense period of activity for the signalman. Resident '5101' Class 'Large Prairie' No 5199 occupies the loop having lifted coaching stock from River Siding.

Below: **LLANGOLLEN GOODS JUNCTION** Sole surviving former LNWR 'Coal Tank' No 58926, resplendent in its BR black livery, is set to depart from Goods Junction for Carrog in 2012. The section starter signal is now located at the western end of the signal box, improvements having commenced towards the end of 2011 resulting in modifications to the track layout and signalling at Goods Junction.

Right: **LLANGOLLEN GOODS JUNCTION** No 70000 *Britannia* restarts its train bound for Carrog during a visit to the railway for the 2012 'Steel, Steam & Stars' event.

Left: **LLANGOLLEN GOODS JUNCTION** The Great Western single-line token exchange equipment, installed at Goods Junction as part of the 2011 remodelling project, can be seen adjacent to the signal box. This equipment allows the footplate crew of an approaching train to deposit the token from the section they are leaving on the 'catcher' and pick up the token for the section ahead, which has been placed in position by the signalman ready for collection.

Above left: **LLANGOLLEN GOODS JUNCTION** After returning to the signal box with the single-line token, the signalman returns the signal lever to normal following the passing of a train from Llangollen.

Left: **LLANGOLLEN GOODS JUNCTION** Resident British Railways Standard Class 4 2-6-4T No 80072 leads a double-headed passenger train towards Llangollen as it leaves the loop, having crossed a westbound train from Llangollen.

Above: **LLANGOLLEN GOODS JUNCTION** Making a westbound departure, this ex-LMS, Stanier 2-6-0 is the sole survivor of its class. Making a guest appearance from its Severn Valley Railway base, the 'Mogul' (a term for locomotives with a 2-6-0 wheel arrangement) carries a 'Corwen Express' headboard, this being a non-stop passenger service along the line.

Above left: **LLANGOLLEN GOODS JUNCTION** Shortly after leaving Llangollen Goods Junction, *Foxcote Manor* is seen with a mixed goods train on what would at first glance appear to be double track. However, the left-hand line nearest the camera leads to Pentrefelin sidings, which today are used for stabling various items of rolling stock; in the past seasonal traffic arriving at Llangollen was held at Pentrefelin, particularly that generated by the local Eisteddfod events.

Above right: **LLANGOLLEN GOODS JUNCTION** Ex-LMS Stanier Class 5 No 44806 leaves Goods Junction with a passenger service; the signalling for the 'up main' and 'loop' lines can clearly be seen behind the train.

Left: **LLANGOLLEN GOODS JUNCTION** A mixed goods train is headed by the sole surviving Caledonian Railway '812' Class locomotive, No 828. Built in 1899 and today based at the Strathspey Railway, the 0-6-0 made a guest appearance at the Llangollen Railway in 2012.

Left: **LLANGOLLEN GOODS JUNCTION**
No 3440 *City of Truro* works away from Goods Junction with a mixed goods train during its 2009 visit to the railway as a participant of the 'Steel, Steam & Stars II' event.

Right: **LLANGOLLEN GOODS JUNCTION** 4-4-0 No 3440 *City of Truro* is seen again but this time with a passenger train at the same location during its 2009 visit for the Betton Grange Society-organised event. Note the different positioning of the loco lamp(s) on these two views, indicating the different train types.

Above: **LLANGOLLEN GOODS JUNCTION** Of all the steam locomotives that once worked on the railways of Britain and survive in preservation today, fate has deemed that those of a former LNER are the least well represented. There were no surviving Peppercorn 'A1' Class 'Pacifics', for example, but the A1 Steam Locomotive Trust took on the seemingly impossible task of building a brand-new example from scratch. Work on the project was duly completed and the locomotive made its first public appearances in steam in 2008. The impressive-looking 4-6-2 carries the number 60163, which follows in sequence from those that were built in the days of steam. Named *Tornado*, No 60163 leaves Llangollen Goods Junction during its 2012 visit to the railway.

Above right: **NEAR PENTREFELIN SIDINGS** The preserved Llangollen Railway crosses the River Dee just once between Llangollen and Corwen. Here resident British Railways Standard Class 4 2-6-4T No 80072 is seen making its way across the Dee Bridge close to the Pentrefelin Sidings complex.

Right: **DEE RIVER BRIDGE** No 7822 *Foxcote Manor* is one of 30 Great Western 'Manor' Class mixed-traffic 4-6-0 locomotives built to a Collett design. The first 20 were built by the GWR between 1938 and 1939, and a final batch of ten emerged following the Second World War and nationalisation, entering traffic in 1950, *Foxcote Manor* being one of this batch. No fewer than nine 'Manors' survived the cutter's torch following the end of steam on Britain's railways, and the Llangollen Railway's resident example is seen here crossing the Dee River Bridge.

DEE RIVER BRIDGE Seen from river level, a mixed goods train makes its way across the bridge headed by LNER 'B1' Class 4-6-0 No 1306, which in preservation carries the name *Mayflower*. Resplendent in the 'Apple Green' livery once associated with the LNER, the 'B1' is one of only two survivors of its class, and visited the railway in 2009.

DEE RIVER BRIDGE Another mixed goods crosses the bridge, on this occasion headed by visiting former Lancashire & Yorkshire Railway Class '27' 0-6-0 No 12322, which dates back to 1896.

BERWYN Having made the climb away from the river crossing, British Railways Standard Class 2 2-6-0 No 78019 approaches the platform at Berwyn station. Following the nationalisation of Britain's railways in 1948, BR set about designing and introducing a range of standard locomotive classes, and these Class 2 2-6-0s became part of the railway scene for the first time in 1953.

Berwyn

Left: **BERWYN** The station's single platform is situated high above the River Dee in a confined location between the river and the busy A5 trunk road. The chain bridge across the river is the third bridge to be located here, the first having been built in 1813 as a means of transporting goods, including coal, from the nearby canal to the then newly built London to Holyhead road. The present-day bridge has been restored in recent years and provides a link between the hotel, the road and the station.

Above: **BERWYN** The sole surviving former London & North Western Railway Webb 'Coal Tank', No 58926, heads a mixed goods train non-stop through the station. The platform is empty apart from the Station Master, who watches as the train passes on a dull and miserable-looking morning.

Left: **BERWYN** Another mixed goods train passes through the station with a locomotive of Great Western pedigree in charge on this occasion, '2800' Class 2-8-0 No 3802. This class was originally introduced in 1903 to a Churchward design, with certain design modifications instigated from 1938 onwards by Charles Collett during his tenure as the GWR's Chief Mechanical Engineer. No 3802 is one of the later Collett locomotives.

BERWYN A non-stop double-headed passenger train passes through the station led by No 78019, an example of the British Railways Standard Class 2 2-6-0 tender locomotives introduced in 1953. The 'Mogul' was visiting the railway from its Great Central Railway base in 2011.

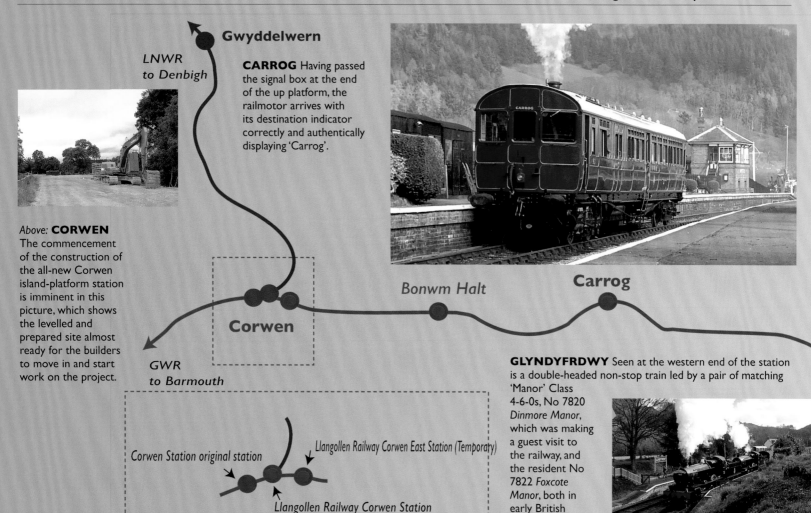

Gwyddelwern

LNWR to Denbigh

CARROG Having passed the signal box at the end of the up platform, the railmotor arrives with its destination indicator correctly and authentically displaying 'Carrog'.

Above: **CORWEN** The commencement of the construction of the all-new Corwen island-platform station is imminent in this picture, which shows the levelled and prepared site almost ready for the builders to move in and start work on the project.

Corwen

GWR to Barmouth

Bonwm Halt

Carrog

GLYNDYFRDWY Seen at the western end of the station is a double-headed non-stop train led by a pair of matching 'Manor' Class 4-6-0s, No 7820 *Dinmore Manor*, which was making a guest visit to the railway, and the resident No 7822 *Foxcote Manor*, both in early British Railways black livery.

Corwen Station original station

Llangollen Railway Corwen East Station (Temporary)

Llangollen Railway Corwen Station Under Construction

Left: **BERWYN** A non-stop double-headed passenger service passes through Berwyn. Llangollen resident Class 4 2-6-4T No 80072, a further example of a British Railways Standard locomotive introduced in the 1950s, leads this train.

Right: **BERWYN** 'Pacific' power here as No 70000 *Britannia* heads another non-stop service at Berwyn.

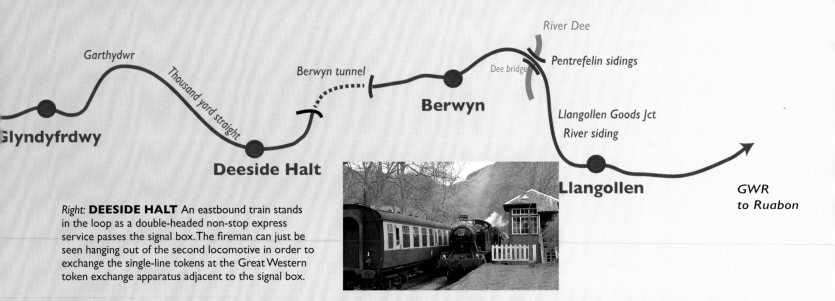

Garthydwr

Thousand yard straight

Berwyn tunnel

River Dee

Dee bridge

Pentrefelin sidings

Berwyn

Glyndyfrdwy

Deeside Halt

Llangollen Goods Jct

River siding

Llangollen

GWR to Ruabon

Right: **DEESIDE HALT** An eastbound train stands in the loop as a double-headed non-stop express service passes the signal box. The fireman can just be seen hanging out of the second locomotive in order to exchange the single-line tokens at the Great Western token exchange apparatus adjacent to the signal box.

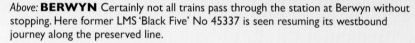

Above: **BERWYN** Certainly not all trains pass through the station at Berwyn without stopping. Here former LMS 'Black Five' No 45337 is seen resuming its westbound journey along the preserved line.

Above right: **BERWYN** Shortly after departing, resident 'Manor' *Foxcote Manor* begins the climb away from the station. There are no fewer than nine surviving 'Manor' Class locomotives out of the total of 30.

Right: **BERWYN** No 246 *Morayshire* is a 'D49' 4-4-0 Class locomotive built for the London & North Eastern Railway at its Darlington Works in 1928. It made a visit to the railway in 2009 from its Bo'ness & Kinneil Railway base and formed part of that year's 'Steal, Steam & Stars' event. Here it undertakes the initial climb away from Berwyn station.

BERWYN TUNNEL
The resident British Railways
Standard 4MT 2-6-4 tank
locomotive emerges from the
689-yard-long Berwyn Tunnel
with a Llangollen-bound train.
The single-bore tunnel is the
only one on today's preserved
Llangollen Railway.

Above: **BERWYN TUNNEL** In 2012 a train approaches the eastern portal of the tunnel headed by an '812' Class 0-6-0 locomotive dating from 1899 and the sole survivor of its class. Normally based on the Strathspey Railway, it initially entered service with the Caledonian Railway and carries that company's impressive-looking blue livery.

Above right: **BERWYN TUNNEL** A mixed goods train is about to enter the tunnel headed by No 6100 *Royal Scot.* The Fowler LMS 'Royal Scot' 4-6-0 locomotives initially appeared on the scene in 1927 with parallel boilers, and William Stanier instigated rebuilds between 1943 and 1955, which included a new boiler, frames and cylinders. *Royal Scot* is seen here on the Llangollen Railway during a 2009 visit.

Right: **BERWYN TUNNEL** A member of the home-based Llangollen Railway fleet of locomotives exits the tunnel here, as GWR '5101' Class 2-6-2T 'Large Prairie' No 5199 heads towards Berwyn and Llangollen. This class of locomotive arrived on the scene in 1929, and No 5199 left Swindon Works new in 1934.

BERWYN TUNNEL *Foxcote Manor* displays a 'Cambrian Coast Express' headboard as it makes progress towards the eastern portal of the tunnel. The positioning of the two lamps above the buffer beam indicates that this train is an 'Express Passenger' working.

Deeside Halt

DEESIDE HALT Shortly after emerging from Berwyn Tunnel, trains heading in a westerly direction arrive at Deeside Halt. A passing loop was initially installed here in 1908, with a signal box to control train movements, but there was never a platform to allow passengers to board or leave trains. A platform was introduced when the Llangollen Railway reached this point in 1990, beyond which the preserved line was extended in 1993.

DEESIDE HALT A Llangollen-bound mixed goods train stands in the loop as a passenger train arrives. The signal box was built by the Llangollen Railway and occupies the position of the original.

1,000 yard straight

Right: **1,000-YARD STRAIGHT** Shortly after leaving Deeside Halt trains encounter what is known locally as the '1,000-yard straight'. No 60163 *Tornado* is certainly a larger, more powerful and heavier locomotive than anything that would have worked regularly along the route during steam days, but made a spectacular impression during its visit to the line as a guest during the 2012 'Steal, Steam & Stars' event.

Below: **1,000-YARD STRAIGHT** A mixed goods train makes its way along the straight, hardly disturbing the sheep in the field as it passes. The fields that adorn the valley beyond the more confined areas closer to Llangollen provide ideal grazing for sheep to supply the area's meat markets with the local speciality, Welsh lamb.

1,000-YARD STRAIGHT A train heads towards Deeside Halt along the '1,000-yard straight', the open nature and scenic beauty of this section of the line being very evident in this image.

1,000-YARD STRAIGHT A double-headed combination comprising two former LMS 'Black Five' 4-6-0s makes progress along the straight. Note that the lead locomotive sports the 'Express Passenger' lamp headcode.

Above: **1,000-YARD STRAIGHT** Another double-headed combination is seen here towards the end of the straight, comprising two locomotives of London & North Western Railway origin. 'G2' Class 'Super D' 0-8-0 No 49395 and 'Coal Tank' No 58926 are today rare examples of surviving LNWR steam locomotive designs.

Right: **1,000-YARD STRAIGHT** This double-header features a couple of locomotives of Great Western heritage; both are of the 'Prairie' 2-6-2T wheel arrangement used extensively by the GWR. The lead locomotive, No 5526, is a member of the '4500' 'Small Prairie' Class while behind is '5101' Class 'Large Prairie' No 5199, working in partnership along the straight.

1,000-YARD STRAIGHT The Great Western railmotor, a unique example of past rail travel in today's preservation scene, makes its way along the straight, crossing a farm bridge as it progresses.

1,000-YARD STRAIGHT This close-up image of the railmotor clearly shows the cylinder and the drive to the wheels of the vehicle's leading bogie.

Above left: **1,000-YARD STRAIGHT** '2800' Class 2-8-0 No 3802, a design of locomotive intended primarily for goods train duties, heads a passenger working along the straight.

Above right: **1,000-YARD STRAIGHT** The 2-8-0 is seen again with the same train as it rounds the curve at the end of this straight section of the Llangollen Railway.

Right: **1,000-YARD STRAIGHT** The scenic splendour of this section of the Llangollen Railway is evident as this Llangollen-bound train rounds the curve on the approach to the straight. The only clue that this is not a steam-era shot is the modern vehicle parked in the field.

Above: **1,000-YARD STRAIGHT** The ex-LNWR 0-8-0 is captured in glorious lighting conditions with a mixed goods train, the type of work this design of locomotive was originally intended to carry out.

Right: **1,000-YARD STRAIGHT** The LNWR 0-8-0s are commonly referred to as 'Super Ds', and this sole surviving example rounds the curve at the end of the straight with its goods working.

Above right: **1,000-YARD STRAIGHT** This Llangollen-bound mixed goods train rounds the curve as it approaches the straight in much duller conditions than those witnessed with the 'Super D' at this location.

1,000-YARD STRAIGHT The Strathspey Railway-based former Caledonian Railway 0-6-0 is seen in a landscape that is not entirely different from that in which it once worked in Scotland. Only the British Railways Mark 1 coaches spoil the illusion, but it is not always possible in railway preservation to bring together items of period rolling stock that would satisfy a Victorian-period locomotive such as No 828, particularly so considering that the 0-6-0 is so far from its original stamping ground.

Garthydwr

Above: **1,000-YARD STRAIGHT** It was a privilege to see Bluebell Railway-based Great Western 'Dukedog' Class 4-4-0 No 9017 on a rare trip away from its Sussex base to a part of Britain in which the class was once found during its working days. The train is seen here towards the end of the 1,000-yard straight.

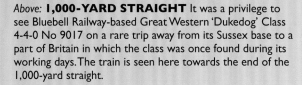

Above right: **APPROACHING GARTHYDWR** After working along the 1,000-yard straight the 'Dukedog' rounds the curve on the approach to the location known as Garthydwr.

Right: **APPROACHING GARTHYDWR** Seen from a higher elevation, 1927 Derby-built 4-6-0 No 6100 *Royal Scot* rounds the curve at the end of the straight.

Left: **APPROACH GARTHYDWR** A typical Great Western Railway branch-line image is seen here with an 0-6-0 pannier tank sandwiched between a pair of auto-train cars. Early British Railways liveries are carried by No 6430 and the two passenger vehicles, which appear to be well loaded with passengers.

Below left: **GARTHYDWR** The former LNWR 'Super D' 0-8-0 is seen with a short mixed goods train, certainly a far lesser load than the 'G2' locomotives were capable of hauling. In their days as part of the British Railways steam locomotive fleet they carried a 7F power classification.

Below: **GARTHYDWR** This wider image at Garthydwr demonstrates why it is one of the most popular photographic locations on the whole of the preserved Llangollen Railway. The pair of locomotives carry the livery of the LNER; leading is 'D49' Class 4-4-0 *Morayshire*, ably assisted by 'B1' Class 4-6-0 No 1306 *Mayflower*.

Above: **GARTHYDWR** *City of Truro* is reputed to have been the first steam locomotive to travel at 100mph, although the achievement was never officially verified. At a much more sedate speed the legendary 4-4-0, today part of the National Collection based at York's National Railway Museum, ambles past.

Right: **GARTHYDWR** The Great Western '5600' Class 0-6-2 tank locomotives built to a Collett design were originally introduced in 1924. In BR days the powerful but comparatively compact locomotives carried a Class 5 mixed-traffic rating and were as much at home on passenger trains as on goods workings.

Above: **GARTHYDWR** No 6100 *Royal Scot* catches the pleasant evening sunlight as it passes with a passenger service.

Above right: **GARTHYDWR** This could justifiably be referred to as 'super power', with *Foxcote Manor* leading No 70000 *Britannia*. The distant signal here relates to the Glyndyfrdwy outer home signal and is permanently fixed in the caution position.

Right: **GARTHYDWR** No 7822 *Foxcote Manor* is working on its own here, and on this occasion is not carrying the 'Express Passenger' lamp code.

Above: **GARTHYDWR** Bearing a 'Corwen Express' headboard, the ultimate destination of this train is without doubt. It is unlikely that any train was ever named the 'Corwen Express' while Corwen was still part of the national rail network, but today in preservation named trains add a little bit of prestige to some services run during major gala events. No 42968 is making a visit from its Severn Valley Railway base.

Right: **GARTHYDWR** The home-based British Railways Standard Class 4 2-6-4T heads a goods train bound for Llangollen. Introduced in 1951, these locomotives were designed at the former Southern Railway's Brighton Works.

GARTHYDWR Another simply timeless image of branch-line activity on the Western Region of British Railways is provided by this shot, which could easily be from the 1950s.

GARTHYDWR Here we see motive power with an LMS pedigree, and two locomotives built to a William Stanier design. No 42968, the sole survivor of its class, is led by a 'Black Five' 4-6-0, of which no fewer than 18 examples have survived the cutter's torch.

GARTHYDWR These two images show the pair of ex-London & North Western Railway locomotives, Webb 'Coal Tank' No 58926 and 'G2' Class 'Super D' 0-8-0 No 49395. In January 1958 the 'Coal Tank' joined forces with 'Super D' No 49121 to haul a Stephenson Locomotive Society special between Abergavenny and Merthyr Tydfil. It was the last passenger train to leave Abergavenny and the occasion was marked at the Llangollen Railway when Nos 49395 and 58926 both visited in 2012. The surviving 'Super D' appears here specially renumbered as No 49121 with the train that ran as the 'Heads of the Valleys Special'.

Above: **GARTHYDWR** This double-headed combination shows a pair of Great Western locomotive types that proved very successful with the GWR and with British Railways following nationalisation. Both the pannier and 'Prairie' tank designs were applied to a number of individual locomotive classes that emerged from Swindon Works over the years.

Below: **GARTHYDWR** The magnificence of Victorian branch-line rail travel in Great Western style is captured once again by the steam railmotor.

Right: **APPROACHING GLYNDYFRDWY** Shortly after passing the fixed distant signal at Garthydwr, the London & North Western Railway pairing approach the Glyndyfrdwy outer home signal.

Below: **APPROACHING GLYNDYFRDWY** The 'G2' Class 0-8-0, which dates from 1921 when it emerged from Crewe Works, heads a mixed goods train as it nears Glyndyfrdwy.

Glyndyfrdwy

GLYNDYFRDWY 2-6-2 'Small Prairie' tank No 4566 stands in the station shortly after arriving with a mixed train from Llangollen.

GLYNDYFRDWY The mixed train was scheduled to make a return trip to Llangollen, and the 'Prairie' tank is seen during its run-round manoeuvre, returning to the station to rejoin the train. The signal box that controlled train movements here in pre-preservation days was located at the end of the up platform on this side of the level crossing, but today's building is beyond the crossing.

Above and above right: **LEAVING GLYNDYFRDWY** A mixed goods train hauled by visiting British Railways Standard Class 2 No 78019 makes progress towards Carrog, having just passed through Glyndyfrdwy. The line runs close by the River Dee as it leaves the station.

Right: **LEAVING GLYNDYFRDWY** This second mixed goods train is led by *City of Truro*, which is sadly no longer a runner and resides as a static exhibit at York's National Railway Museum. As it heads towards Carrog it passes the Glyndyfrdwy distant signal, which is fixed at caution.

Above: **LEAVING GLYNDYFRDWY** The river is clearly seen in this early springtime shot with the trees not yet carrying their full leaf cover. The British Railways Standard Class 4 tank locomotive is matched with the carmine-and-cream-liveried Mark 1 coaching stock, a colour scheme often referred to as 'blood and custard'.

Above right: **LEAVING GLYNDYFRDWY** The Didcot Railway Centre-based railmotor passes the Glyndyfrdwy distant signal, partly obscured by its exhaust, with the valley side rising high in the background.

Right: **LEAVING GLYNDYFRDWY** The former London & North Western Railway pairing is captured shortly after passing the fixed distant signal.

LEAVING GLYNDYFRDWY A dramatic head-on shot captures No 7822 *Foxcote Manor* as the 4-6-0 makes progress bound for Carrog.

Carrog

Right: **CARROG** is a fine example of a sleepy Great Western country station. Looking west, trains pass under the road bridge as they head for Corwen. The total running length of the Llangollen Railway became 10 miles when the route was reopened as far as Corwen in 2014.

Below: **CARROG** The section starter signal can just be seen behind the train as the Caledonian Railway 0-6-0 is seen arriving at Carrog. The Llangollen Railway opened the extension between Glyndyfrdwy and Carrog in 1996.

Above: **CARROG** Following its journey along the Dee Valley from Glyndyfrdwy, the LNWR 'Coal Tank' passes the home signal post as it arrives at Carrog with a goods train. The signal indicates that this train is to arrive in the up platform, which features the main station building.

Above right: **CARROG** The signal is passed in the opposite direction by '5101' Class 'Prairie' tank No 5199 as it leaves Carrog bound for Llangollen.

Right: **CARROG** Having passed the signal box at the end of the up platform, the railmotor arrives with its destination indicator correctly and authentically displaying 'Carrog'.

Above: **CARROG** No 80072 arrives with its train; the diesel locomotive will be attached to the rear. Because the temporary single-platform Corwen East station has no run-round facilities, trains bound for there either feature a specially converted coach to allow push-pull running, or a locomotive is attached to the rear of the train at Carrog for the safe operation of the return journey.

Above right: **CARROG** Prepared specially for a '1960s' event, *Foxcote Manor* passes the signal box in the guise of a work-worn No 7807 *Compton Manor*, a member of the class long since scrapped.

Right: **CARROG** The scenic surroundings of the station are evident as a double-headed working from Llangollen arrives.

Above: **CARROG** A Llangollen-bound departure is made, with No 1744, a Nigel Gresley-designed former Great Northern Railway 'N2' Class 0-6-2 tank locomotive, at the head of the train. This locomotive was visiting the railway from its Great Central Railway base.

Above right: **CARROG** Passing under the road bridge, *Foxcote Manor* departs for Corwen. In 2013, prior to the railway extending services to Corwen the following year, trains began running as far as Bonwm Halt. Although the halt no longer exists, the Great Western Railway originally introduced a stopping point at the location in 1935.

Right: **LEAVING CARROG** Although services did not actually officially commence to the west of Carrog until 2013, trains ran topped-and-tailed along the already laid section of track during the 2012 staging of the 'Steal, Steam & Stars' event. *Tornado* was a guest during the event and is seen shortly after departing from Carrog, the very clean looking ballast being indicative of the fact that this section of track was not yet in constant use.

APPROACHING CARROG The train seen behind *Tornado* makes its return with the ex-GNR 'N2' 0-6-2T in charge. The signal is already fully operational and indicates to the crew that all is satisfactory to proceed and enter the station.

LEAVING CARROG This train, headed by pannier tank No 6430, is seen leaving Carrog for Corwen in 2016, some three years after trains had started running regularly to the west of Carrog.

HEADING FOR CORWEN Visiting 'Manor' Class 4-6-0 No 7820 *Dinmore Manor* runs close by the River Dee with a Corwen-bound train from Carrog.

HEADING FOR CORWEN, No 5199 proceeds with caution as it approaches a farm crossing.

HEADING FOR CORWEN A 'Cambrian Coast Express' headboard is carried by *Foxcote Manor*, together with an 'Express Passenger' headlamp code. The early British Railways black livery matches perfectly the 1950s carmine and cream colour scheme of the BR Mark 1 coaches behind the tender.

Corwen East

CORWEN EAST No 80072 arrives at the temporary wooden platform structure that allows passengers to board and disembark until the new Llangollen Railway Corwen station has been built and brought into use.

Corwen

Right: **CORWEN** The site for the all-new Corwen island platform station has been levelled and prepared ready for the builders to move in and start work.

Below: **CORWEN** Adjacent to the site of the new station, the tree line and former trackbed of the LNWR route to Denbigh curve away to the north.

Below right: **CORWEN** Access to the original Corwen station site is no longer practical due to the raising of a road that was previously crossed by a bridge to the east of the station. If a bridge was put in place today there would not be sufficient clearance for the height of some of the vehicles that now regularly use the much busier road.

Index

Further reading

• A PAST AND PRESENT COMPANION •

THE GREAT WESTERN IN NORTH WALES

• John Hillmer & Paul Shannon •

Including the Llangollen, Bala Lake, Fairbourne railways

Features over 50 locations including:
Ruabon • Llangollen • Bala • Blaenau Ffestiniog • Dolgellau • Barmouth

Including the Llangollen Railway, the Bala
Lake Railway and the Fairbourne Railway,
this is the ideal travelling companion
for visitors to the former GWR lines
Heritage Railways in North Wales

The Great Western in North Wales		
ISBN 978 1 85895 255 0	Softcover	£16.99